D0327231

Where
dogs
dream

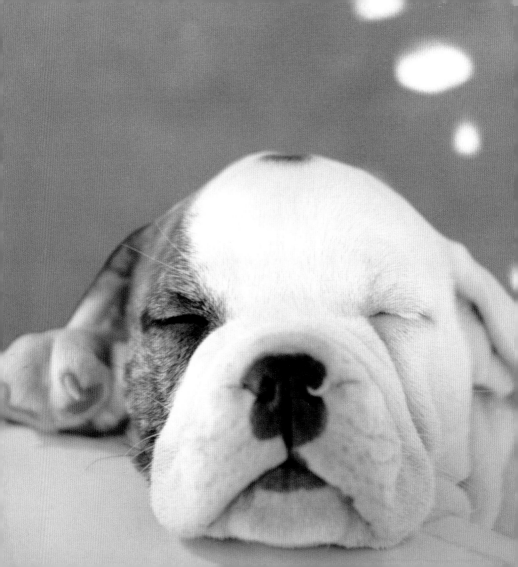

Where
dogs
dream

Edited by Kit Whitfield

BARRON'S

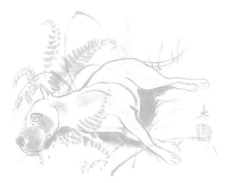

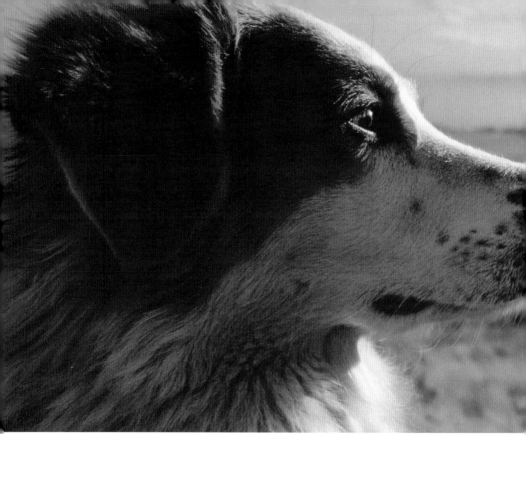

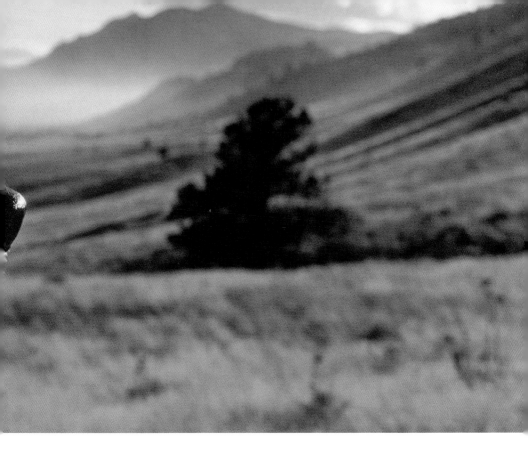

What is the color of the wind?

Zen saying

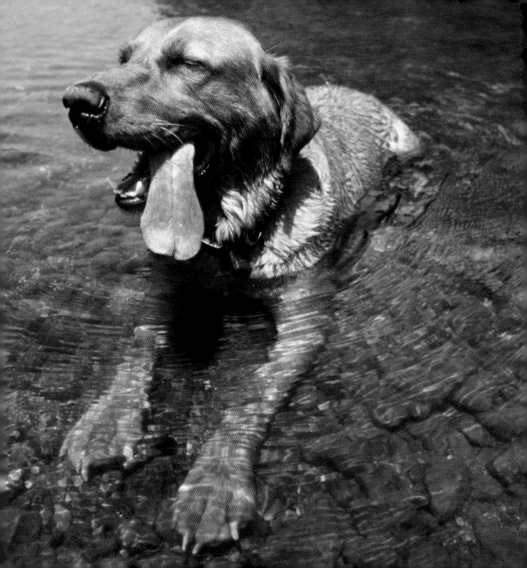

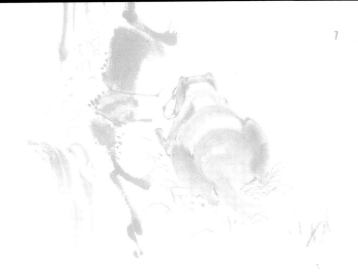

I'll take all the time I please this afternoon
before leaving my place alongside this river.
It pleases me, loving rivers.
Loving them all the way back to their source.
Loving everything that increases me.

Raymond Carver

The clearest way into the Universe is through a forest wilderness.

John Muir

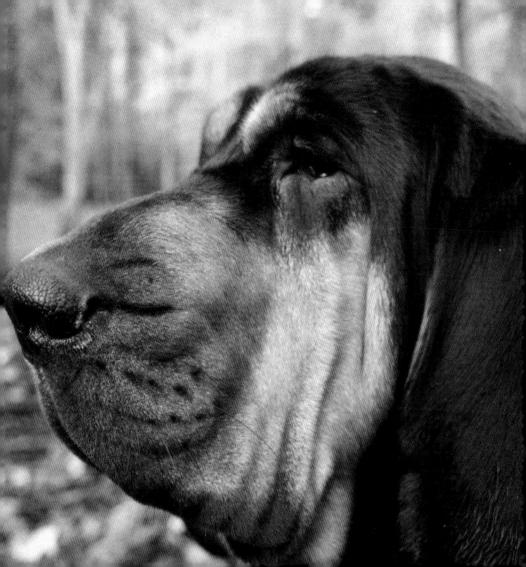

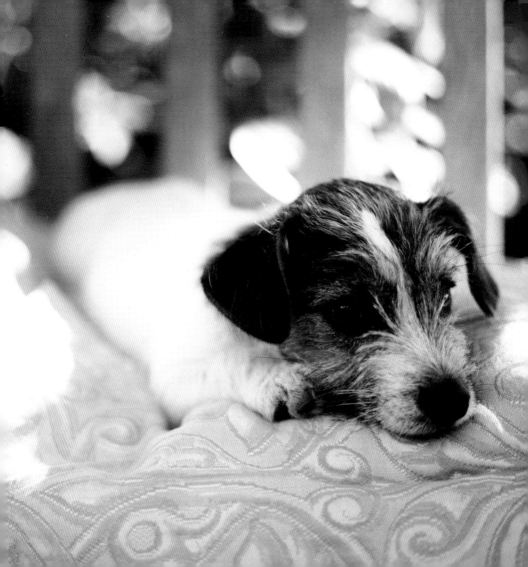

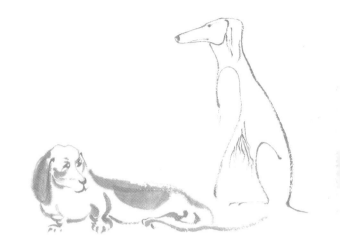

There are days when I wonder what it feels like to be fully awake.

Verlyn Klinkenborg

O there is blessing in this gentle breeze,
A visitant that while it fans my cheek
Doth seem half-conscious of the joy it brings
From the green fields, and from yon azure sky.

William Wordsworth

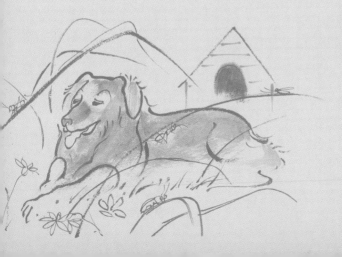

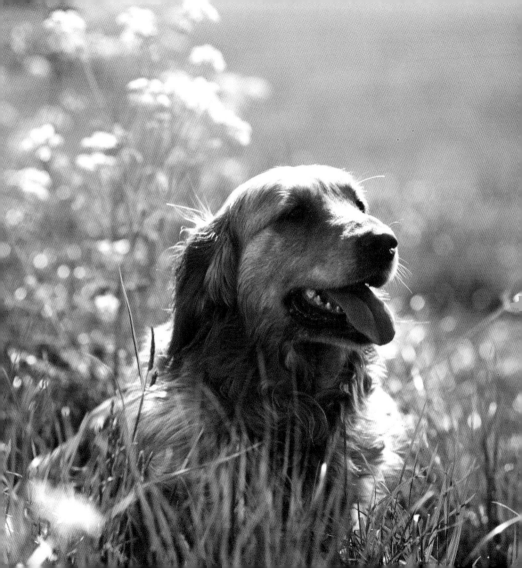

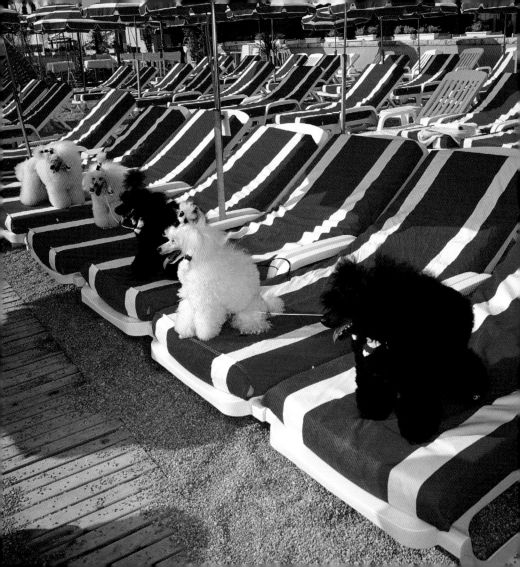

...color everywhere, and music, and amazing luxury— one can imagine how wonderful this crowded and vivid existence would seem...

St. John Lucas

Beneath an uncaged sky
My imagination stirs...

Pat Moon

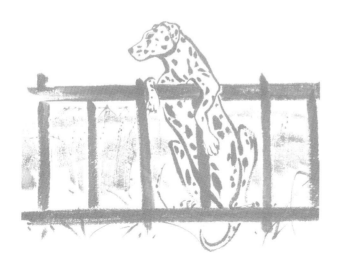

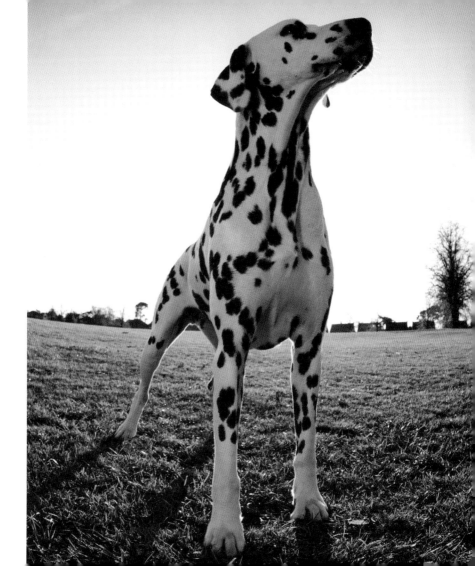

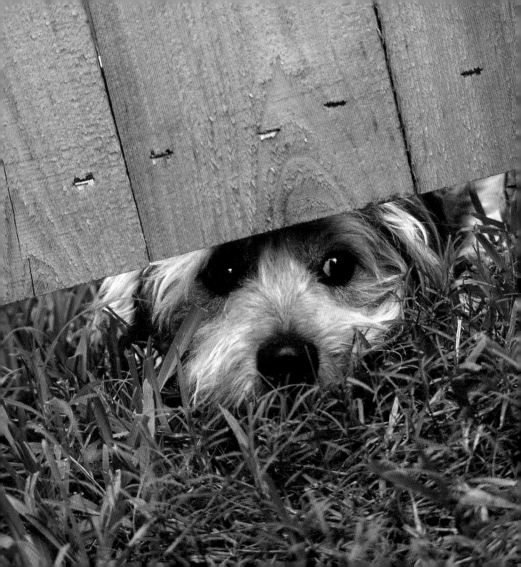

They might not need me—yet they might—
I'll let my Heart be just in sight—
A smile so small as mine might be
Precisely their necessity—

Emily Dickinson

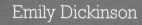

**increasing heat
locusts and the neighbors
raise their voices**

Karen Sohne

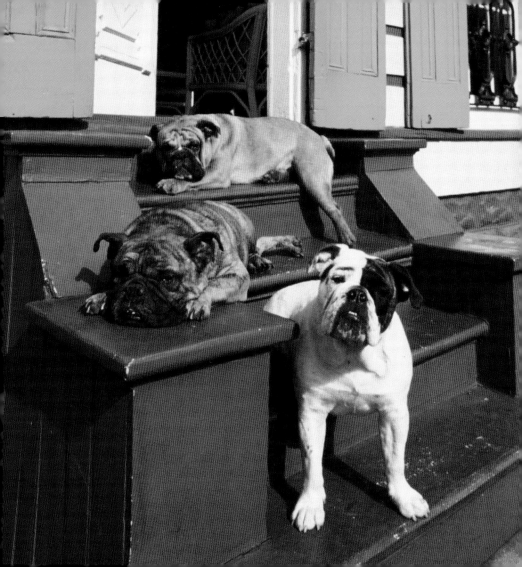

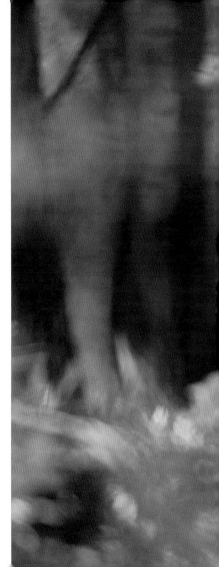

Who lived in these
ancient woods?
Many thousand years
ago small men made
their dwelling here

Jean Kenward

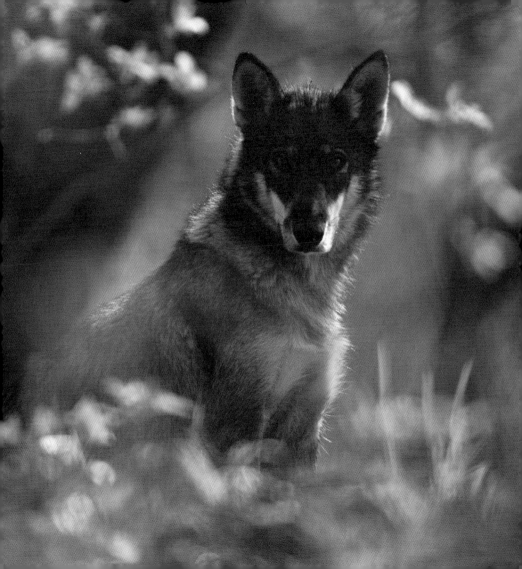

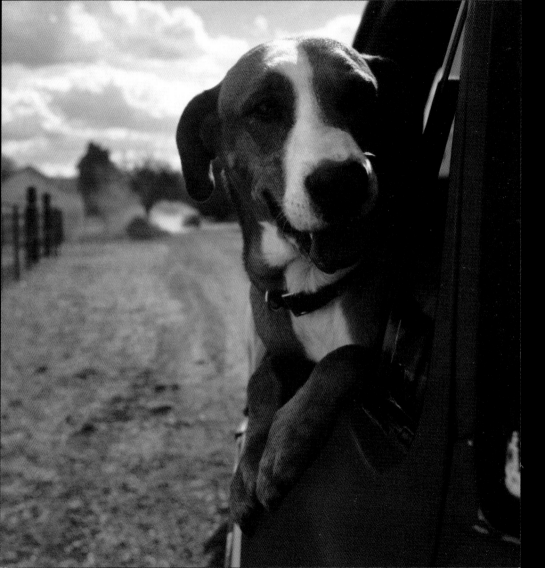

On and on we sped, as through a mighty sea,
cross-hatched with lines and shadows,
our nostrils flaring in the windy mist.
The landscape rumbled to our engine's roar,
and my heart sang an ode impossible to repeat.

Paolo Buzzi

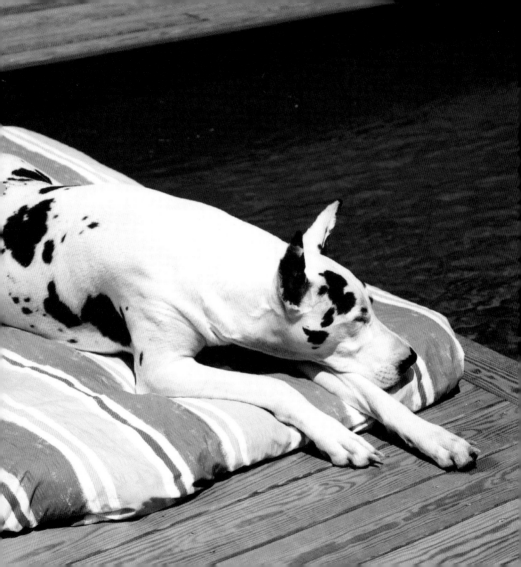

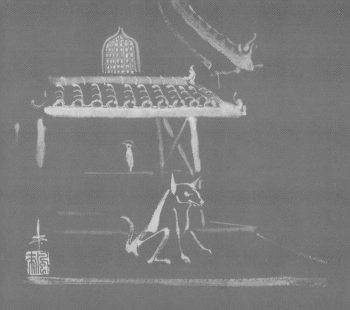

And I will rest and dream and sit on the deck
Watching the world go by...

Carl Sandburg

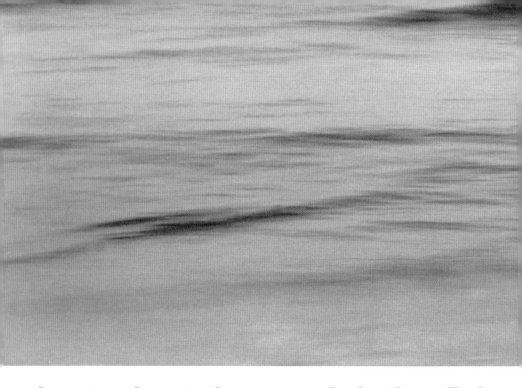

I must go down to the seas again, for the call of the running tide
Is a wild call and a clear call that may not be denied;

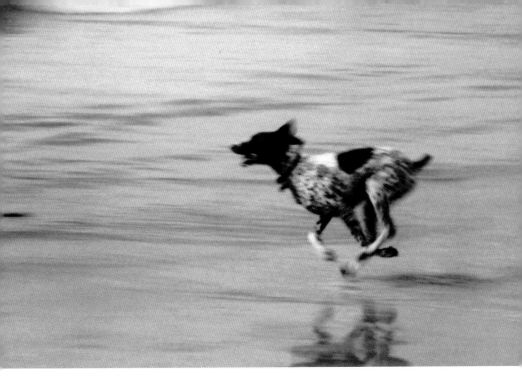

And all I ask is a windy day with the white clouds
 flying,
And the flung spray and the blown spume, and the
 sea-gulls crying.

John Masefield

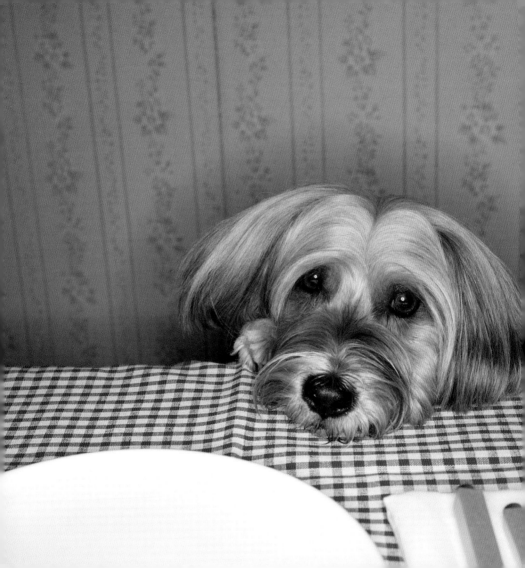

Give me a good digestion, Lord, And also something to digest...

Author unknown

Listen to the golden grasshopper chirping
In the magic garden!
Listen to the cricket! Singing in the forest
Where the souls of the ancients chant through
   dove-calls,
Listen to the soil as it charms its children!

Faustin Charles

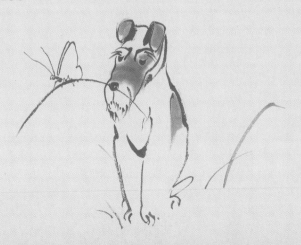

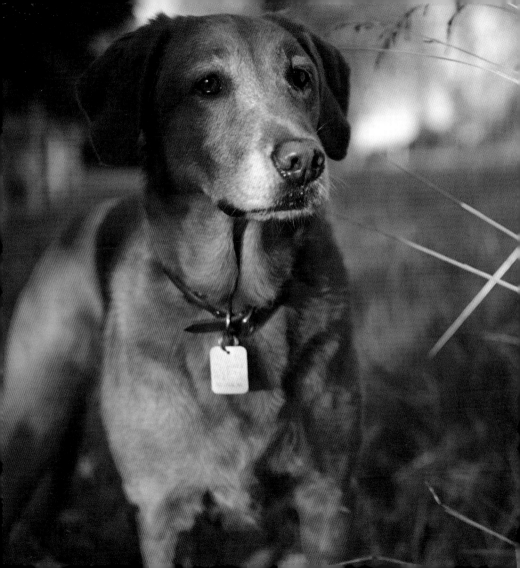

Cloud maps shift across a windy sky, as unknown countries ebb and flow.

Francis Howell

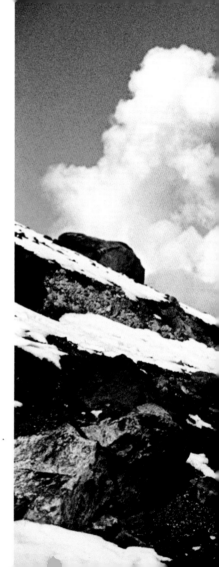

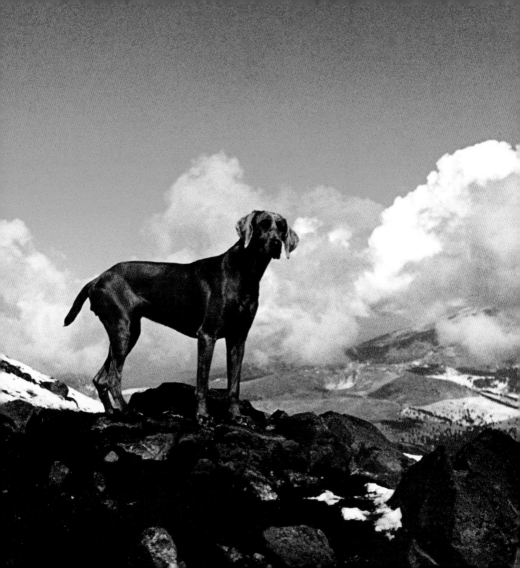

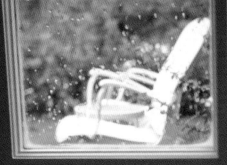

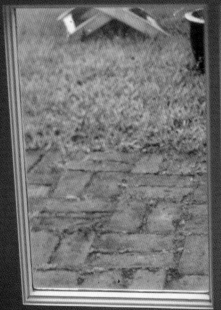
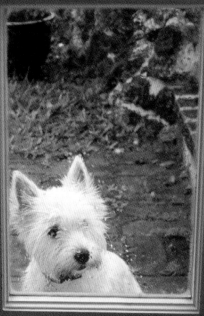

When one door of happiness closes, another opens, but often we look so long at the closed door that we do not see the one which has been opened for us.

Helen Keller

I cannot think of anything today
That I would rather do than be myself,
Primevally alive, and have the sun
Shine into me...

Edwin Arlington Robinson

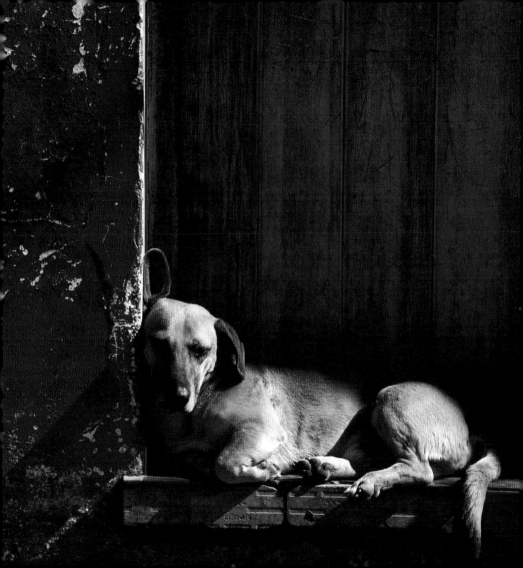

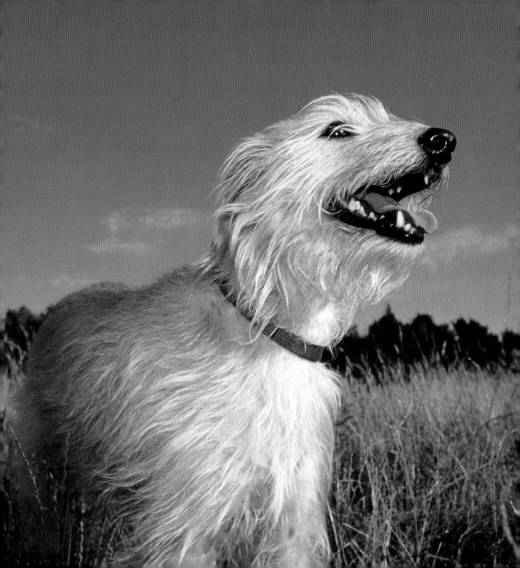

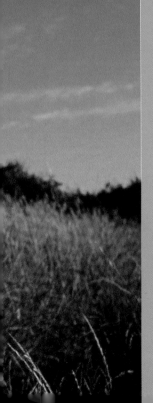

The sun is mine
And the trees are mine
The light breeze is mine
And the birds that inhabit the air
are mine
Their voices upon the wind
are in my ear...

Robert Hogg

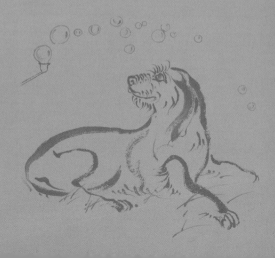

I shall outdream the slumber of the hills,
I am the bud, the flower, I the seed...

John Spencer Muirhead

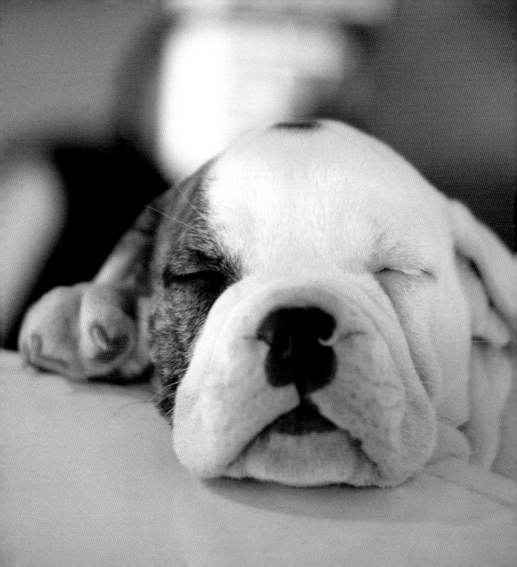

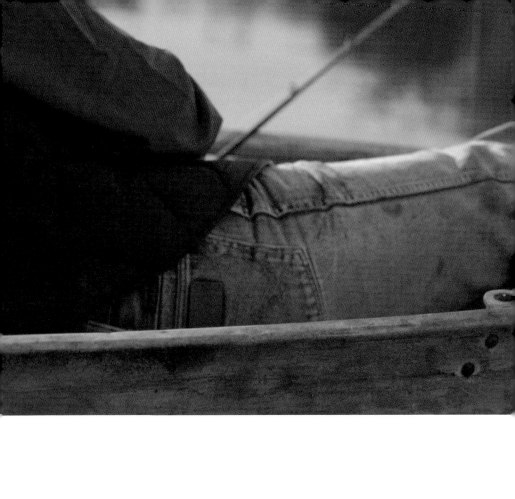

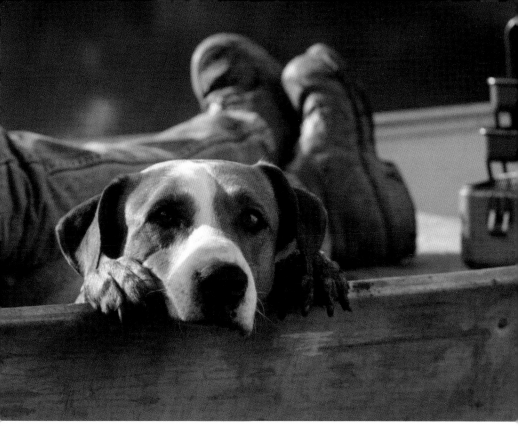

I wonder if the spirit of the water has anything to say.

Carol Ann Duffy

The dew is gleaming on the grass,
 The morning hours are seven,
And I am fain to watch you pass,
 Ye soft white clouds of heaven.

Archibald Lampman

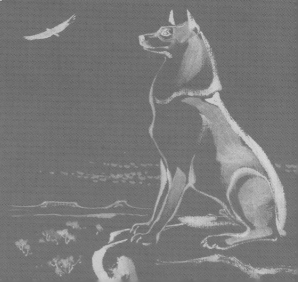

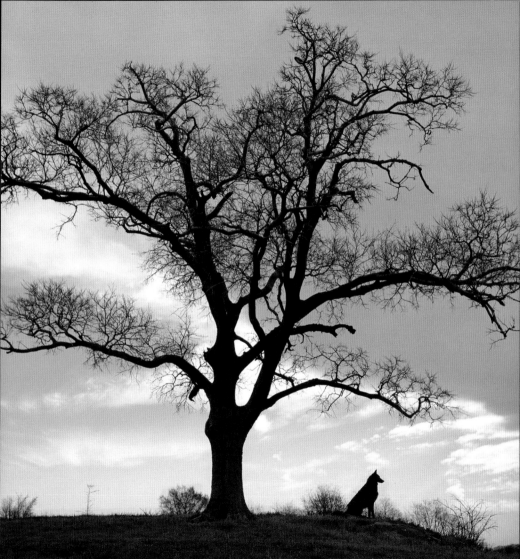

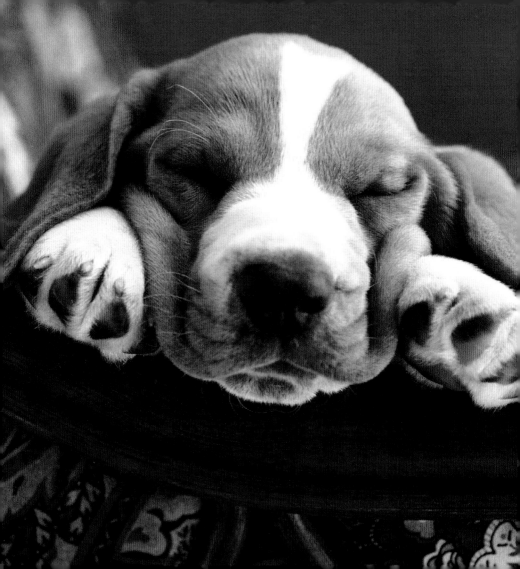

My kingdom of childhood sleep was vast...
I was certain that just over the threshold of
my own sleep lay the world meant for me.

Andrei Codrescu

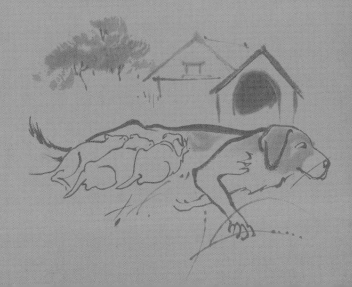

dreaming of forests
I gaze at a paper on the wood floor
sunlight shines through the varnish.

Kit Whitfield

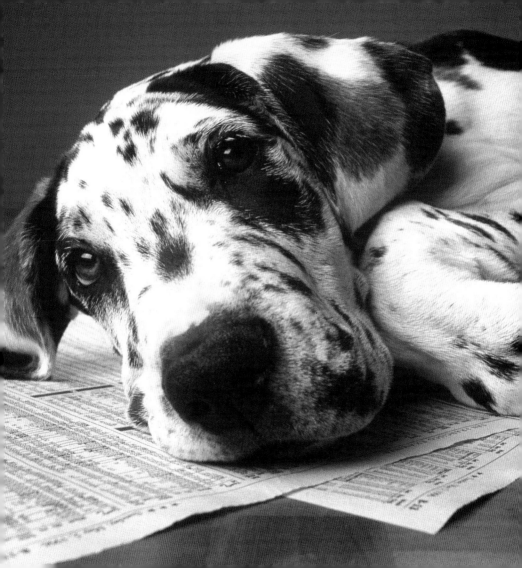

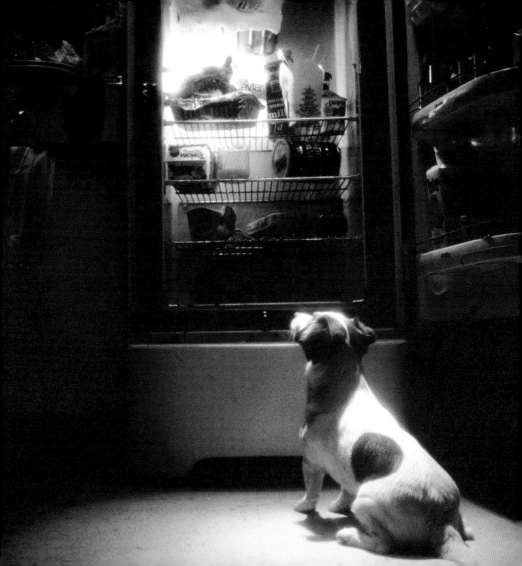

Dreams are the soul's pantry. Keep it well stocked and your soul will never hunger.

Cindy Williams

Today I think
Only with scents, —scents dead
	leaves yield,
And bracken, and wild carrot's seed...

Edward Thomas

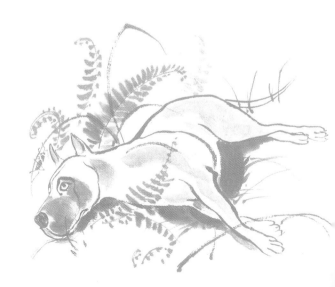

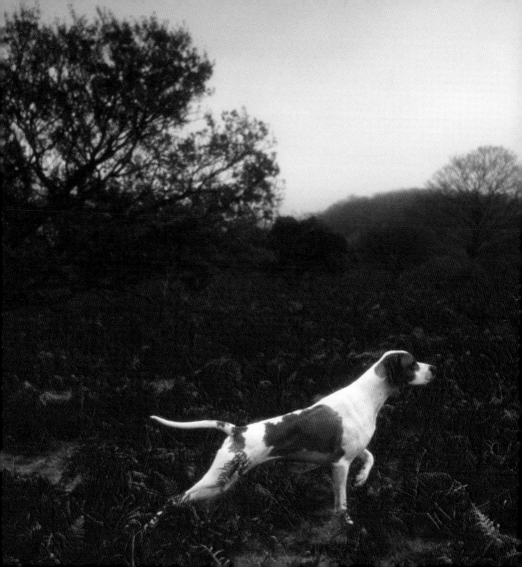

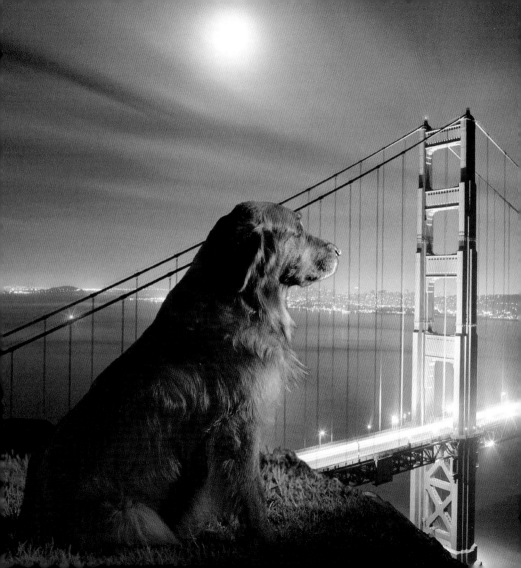

The river, slipping between
Lamps, is rayed with golden bands
Half way down its heaving sides;
Revealed where it hides.

Under the bridge
Great electric cars
Sing through, and each with a floor-light racing
   along at its side.
Far off, oh, midge after midge
Drifts over the gulf that bars
The night with silence, crossing the lamp-
   touched tide.

D. H. Lawrence

Come play with me;
Why should you run...?
When all I would do
Is to scratch your head
And let you go.

W. B. Yeats

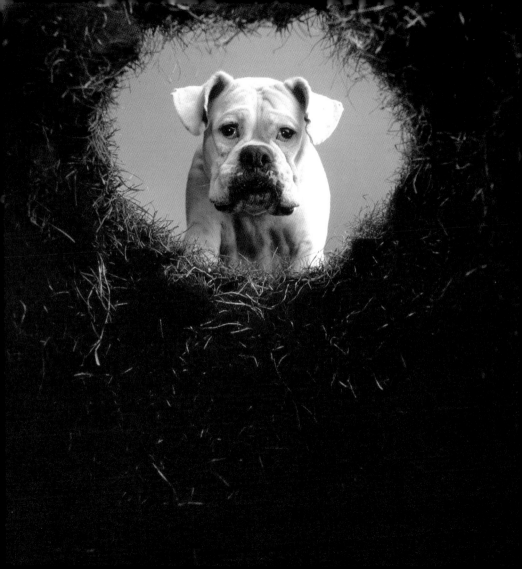

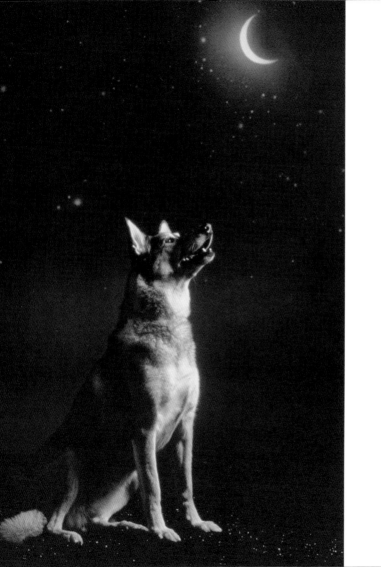

Look at the stars! look, look up at the skies!
O look at all the fire-folk sitting in the air!

Gerard Manley Hopkins

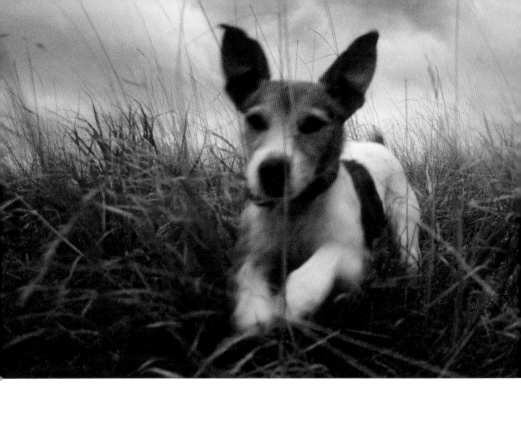

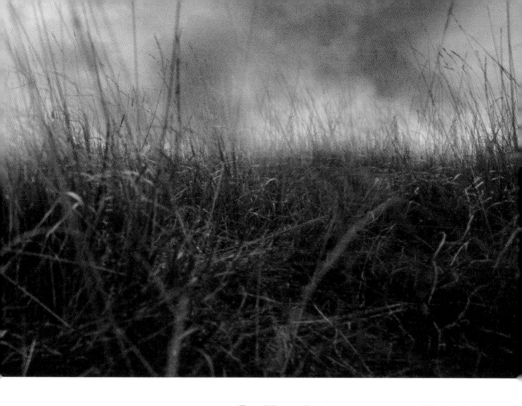

Galloping across fields
With nowhere to go but home
And happy for it.

Adele David

Where lies the land to which the ship would go?
Far, far ahead, is all her seamen know.
And where the land she travels from? Away,
Far, far behind, is all that they can say.

Arthur Hugh Clough

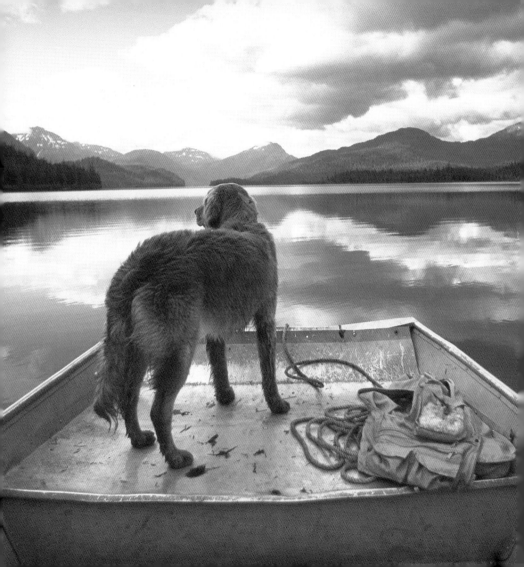

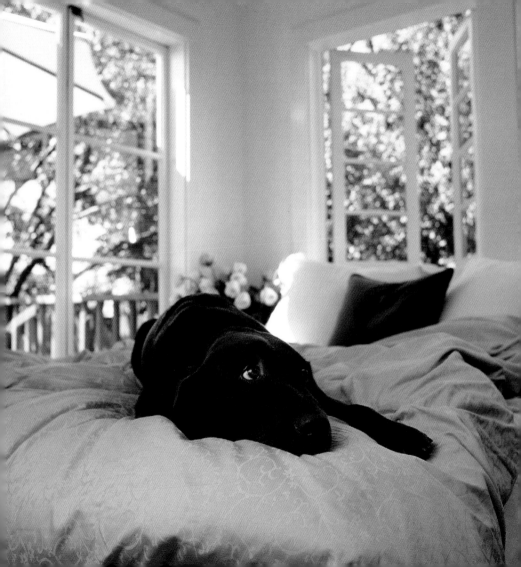

cold saturday—
drawn back into bed
by my own warmth

John Stevenson

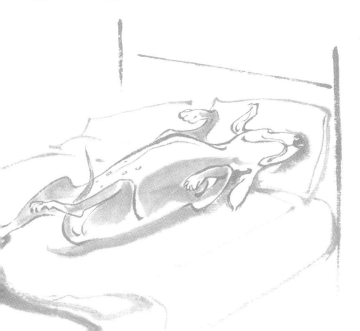

Fall, leaves, fall; die, flowers, away;
Lengthen night and shorten day;
Every leaf speaks bliss to me
Fluttering from the autumn tree.

Emily Brontë

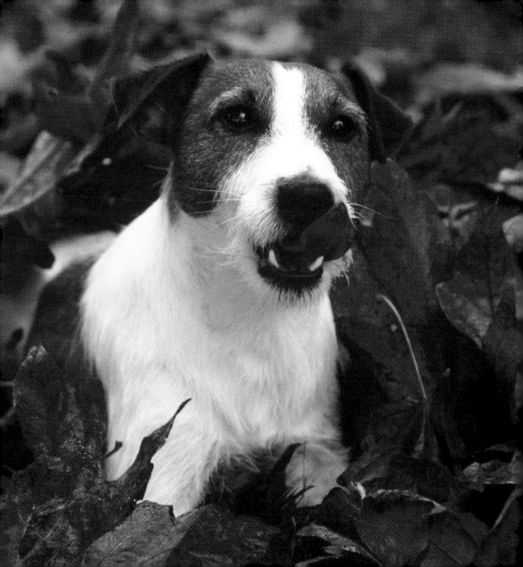

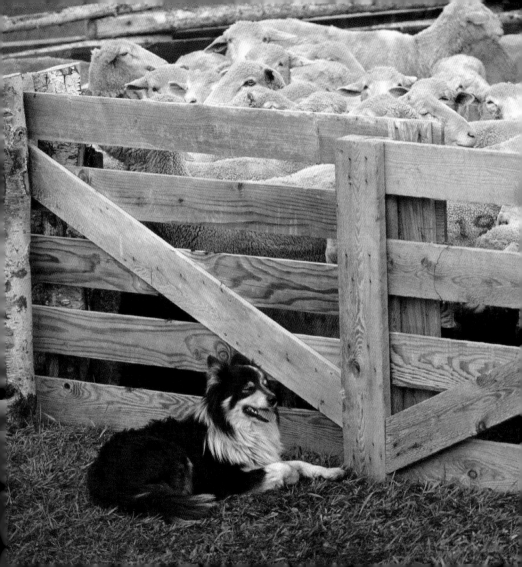

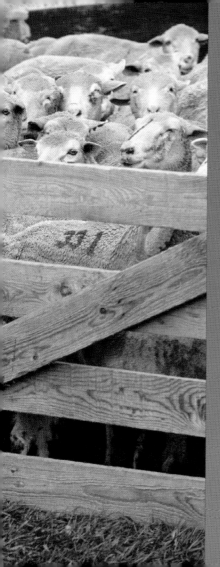

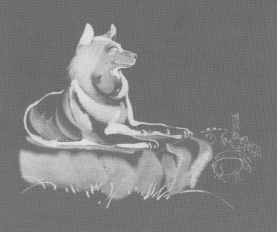

**summer haze
the sheep voices
sing harmonies.**

Kit Whitfield

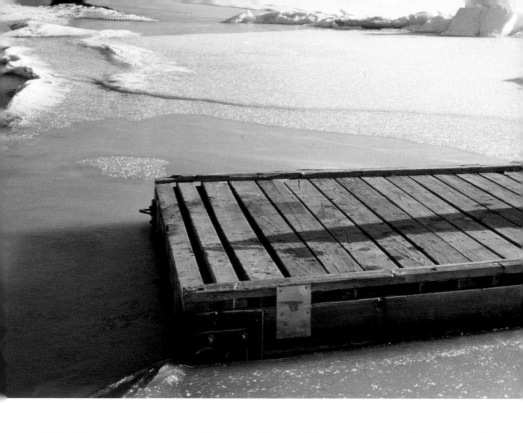

Night, snow, and sand make up the form of
    my thin country,
all silence lies in its long line,

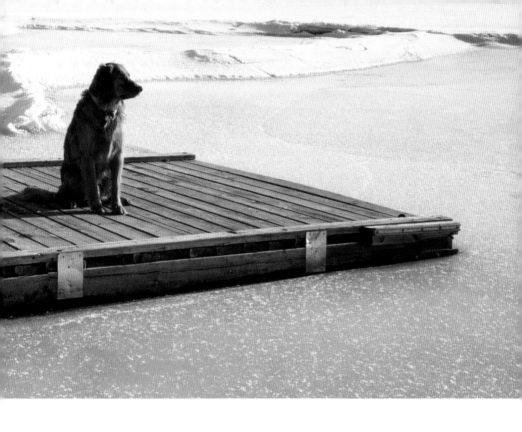

all foam flows from its marine beard,
all coal covers it with mysterious kisses.

Pablo Neruda

A neighborhood.
At dusk.

Things are getting ready
to happen
out of sight.

Eavan Boland

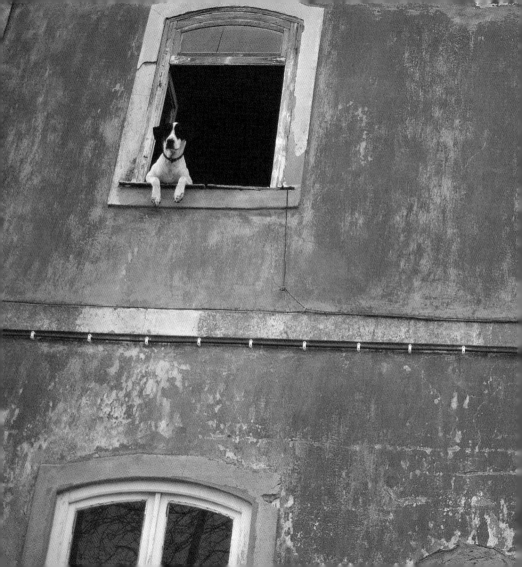

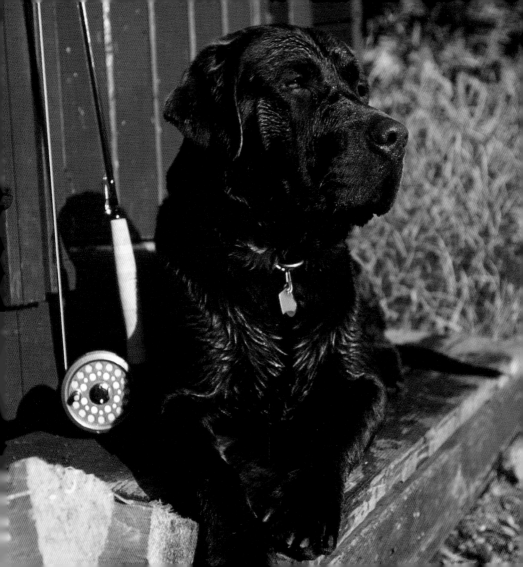

casting off the lines
    odor from the wooden wharf
       of drying dew

Robert Speiss

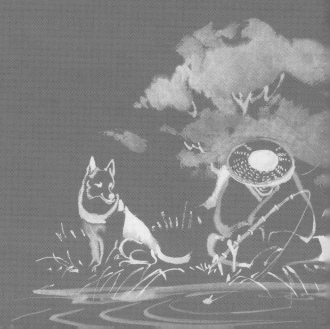

Sail forth! steer for the deep waters only!
Reckless, O soul, exploring, I with thee, and
　thou with me;
For we are bound where mariner has not yet
　dared to go,
And we will risk the ship, ourselves and all.

O my brave soul!
O farther, farther sail!
O daring joy, but safe! Are they not all the seas
　of God?
O farther, farther, farther sail!

Walt Whitman

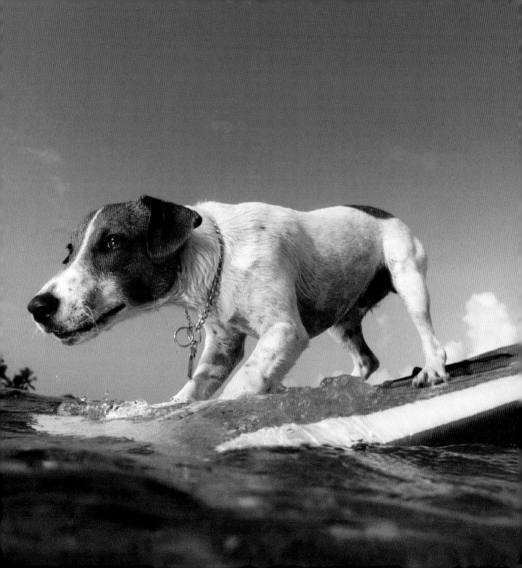

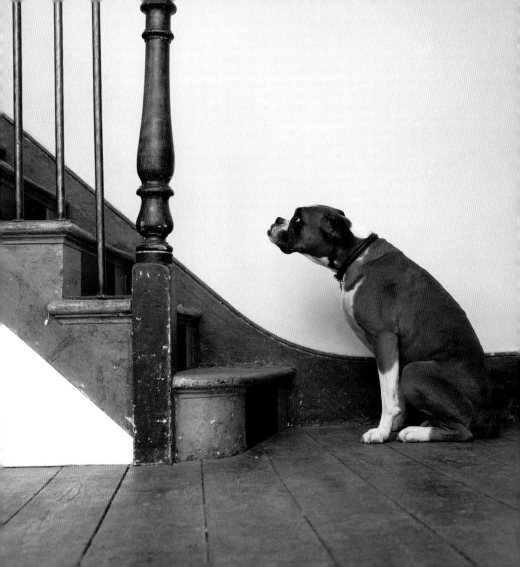

Somebody is whispering on the stair.
What are those words, half spoken, half
   drawn back?
Whence are those muffled words, some red,
   some black?
Who is whispering? Who is there?

Harold Monro

Awakening...
the cold fresh scent:
new snow.

Anita Virgil

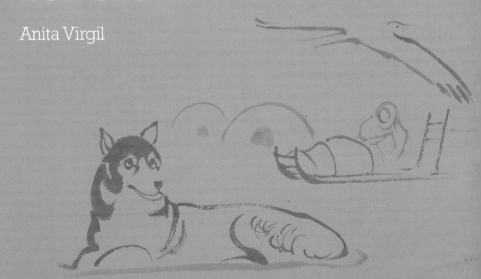

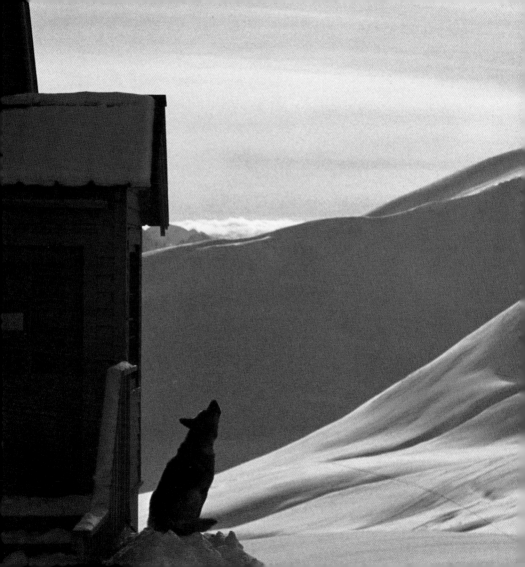

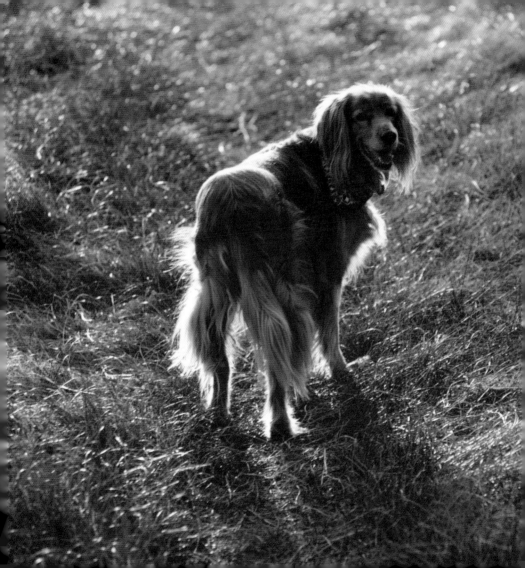

wind in the sagebrush— the same dusty color the smell of it

Elizabeth Searle Lamb

This quiet morning light
reflected, how many times
from grass and trees and clouds
enters my north room
touching the walls with
grass and clouds and trees.

William Carlos Williams

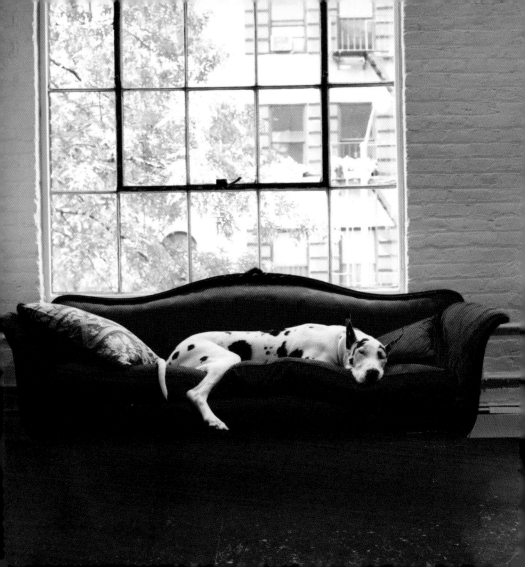

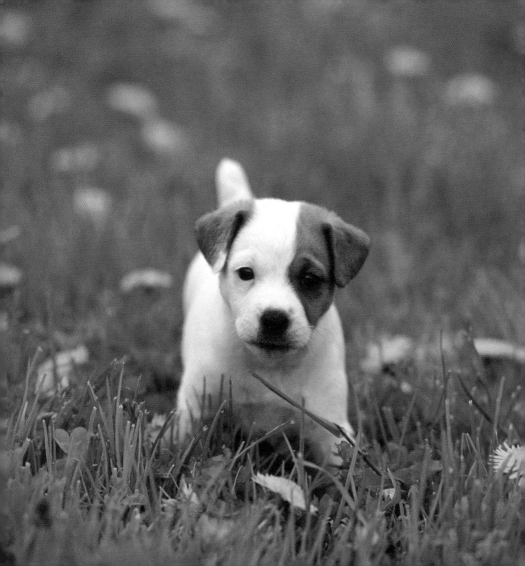

coming home
flower
by
flower

Jane Reichhold

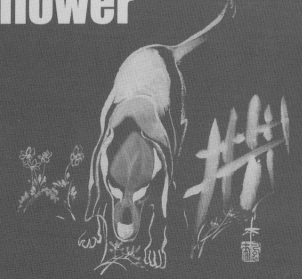

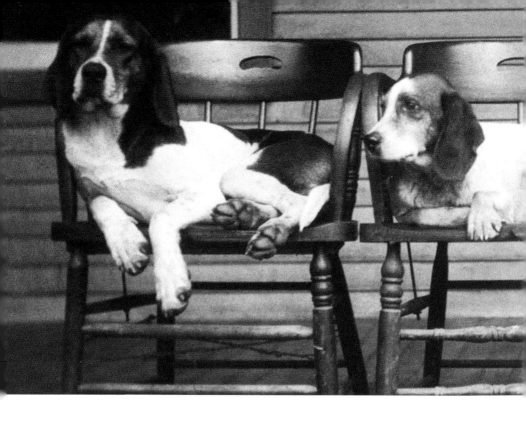

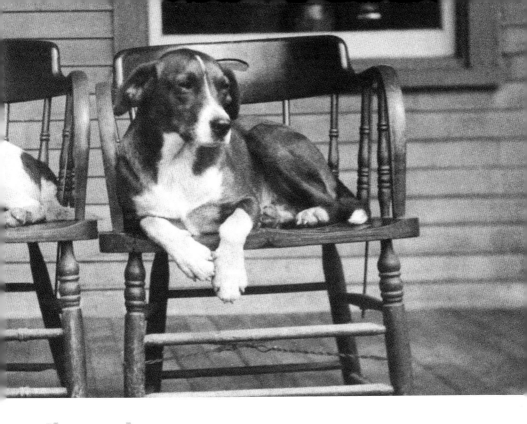

on the porch
in mold-speckled pine needles
my waiting for you

Jane Reichhold

What's there, beyond? A thing
   unsearched and strange;
Not happier, but different. Something vast
And new. Some unimaginable change
From what has been. Perchance the end
   at last?

Edward Bulwer Lytton

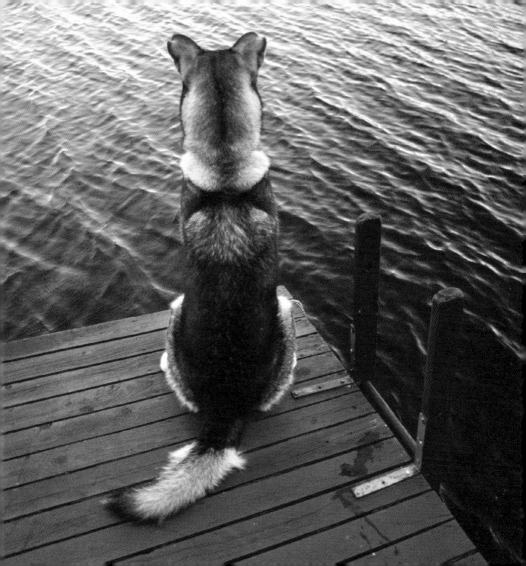

Acknowledgments

p.7 Excerpt from "Where Water Comes Together with Other Water" by Raymond Carver, copyright © 1984, 1985 by Raymond Carver. Used by permission of Random House, Inc. p.15 Excerpt from *The Oxford Book of French Verse* by St. John Lucas (Clarendon, 1920). Reprinted by permission of Oxford University Press. p.16 Excerpt from "Tiger in a Zoo" by Pat Moon from her *Earthlines* (Pimlico, 1991). Copyright © 1991 by Pat Moon. Used by permission of the author. p.20 "increasing heat" by Karen Sohne from *Haiku World: An International Poetry Almanac* (Kodansha International, 1996). Used by permission of the author. p.22 Excerpt from "The Flint" by Jean Kenward from *Otherworlds* ed. Judith Nicholls (Faber & Faber, 1995). Copyright © 1995 by Jean Kenward. p.25 Excerpt from "Highway to the Stars" by Paolo Buzzi. p.27 Excerpt from "Waiting" in *Chicago Poems* by Carl Sandburg. Copyright 1916 by Holt, Rinehard and Winston and renewed 1944 by Carl Sandburg. Reprinted by permission of Harcourt, Inc. p.28/29 Excerpt from "Sea Fever" by John Masefield from his *John Masefield: Poems* (Heinemann, 1923). Used by permission of The Society of Authors as the Literary Representative of the Estate of John Masefield. p.32 Excerpt from "Landscape" by Faustin Charles. p.34 "Cloud maps" by Francis Howell. Used by permission of the author. p.37 Helen Keller. Courtesy of the American Foundation for the Blind, Helen Keller Archives. p.38 Excerpt from "Captain Craig: II" by Edwin Arlington Robinson from his *Collected Poems of Edwin A. Robinson* (Macmillan, 1921). p.45 Excerpt from "Selling Manhattan" by Carol Ann Duffy from her *Selected Poems*. p.49 Excerpt from "The Blessed Waters of Sleep" by Andrei Codrescu from his *The Dog with the Chip in His Neck* (St. Martin's Press, 1999). Used by permission of the author. p.58 Excerpt from "To a Squirrel at Kyle-na-no" by W. B. Yeats. Used by permission of A. P. Watt Ltd. on behalf of Michael B. Yeats. p.63 "Hare" by Adele David from *A Footprint on the Air: An Anthology of Nature Verse* ed. Naomi Lewis (Hutchinson Junior Books, 1983). Copyright © 1983 by Adele David. Used by permission of the author. p.67 "cold saturday" by John Stevenson from *The Haiku Anthology* ed. Cor van den Heuvel (W. W. Norton and Company, 1999). p.72/73 Excerpt from "Discoverers of Chile" translated by Anthony Kerrigan, from *Pablo Neruda: Selected Poems*, edited by Nathaniel Tarn, published by Jonathan Cape. Reprinted by permission of The Random House Group Ltd. p.74 Excerpt from "This Moment" by Eavan Boland from his *Collected Poems*. Copyright © 1995 by Eavan Boland. p.77 "casting off" by Robert Speiss from *Haiku: Poetry Ancient and Modern* ed. Jackie Hardy (MQ Publications Ltd., 2002). Used by permission of Lee Gurga, Literary Executor. p.81 Excerpt from "Rumour" by Harold Monro from his *Collected Poems*, (Cobden-Sanderson, 1933). Used by permission of Gerald Duckworth & Co. Ltd. p.82 "Awakening" by Anita Virgil from her *A 2nd Flake*. Copyright © 1974 by Anita Virgil. p.85 "wind" by Elizabeth Searle Lamb from *Across the Windharp: Collected and New Haiku* (La Almeida Press, 1999). Copyright © 1999 by Elizabeth Searle Lamb. Used by permission of the author. p.86 Excerpt from "To Mark Anthony in Heaven" by William Carlos Williams, from his *Collected Poems: 1909-1939*, Volume I (Carcanet Press). Copyright © 1938 by New Directions Publishing Corp. Reprinted by permission of New Directions Publishing Corp. and Pollinger Ltd. p.89 "coming home" and p.91 "on the porch" by Jane Reichhold from her *A Dictionary of Haiku: Classified by Season, Words, and Traditional Modern Methods* (AHA Books, 1992). Copyright © 1992 by Jane Reichhold. Used by permission of the author.

Photo Credits

First edition for North America published in 2003 by
Barron's Educational Series, Inc.

Copyright © MQ Publications Ltd 2003

All inquiries should be addressed to:
Barron's Educational Series, Inc.
250 Wireless Boulevard
Hauppauge, New York 11788
http://www.barronseduc.com

International Standard Book No. 0-7641-5640-3

Library of Congress Catalog Card No. 2002110038

Series Editor: Leanne Bryan
Design: Balley Design Associates
Illustrations: André Sollier

Printed in China
9 8 7 6 5 4 3 2